THE BIBLE
DIVINE OR HUMAN?

The Bible: Divine or Human?
Evidence of Biblical Infallibility and Support for Building Your Life and Nation on Biblical Truth

By Stephen McDowell

Copyright © 2016 by Stephen McDowell
Second Print, January 2025

This book is reprinted by American Family Association with permission of Stephen McDowell and Providence Foundation.

Providential Perspective Series 17
All rights reserved. No part of this book may be reproduced in any manner whatso-ever without written permission of the publisher, except in the case of brief quota-tions in articles and reviews.

Published by:
Providence Foundation
PO Box 6759
Charlottesville, VA 22906
434-978-4535
Email: info@providencefoundation.com
www.providencefoundation.com

The Providence Foundation is a Christian educational organization whose purpose is to train and network leaders of education, business, and politics to transform their culture for Christ, and to teach all citizens how to disciple nations. The Bibli-cal Worldview University provides training for leaders of all ages and spheres of life in a curriculum of real-world topics, offered via distance learning (on DVD, CD, and/or print) and on-line in multiple languages. Live classes are also offered throughout the year in Charlottesville and other parts of the world.

The *Providential Perspective* is a regular publication of the Providence Foundation and contains contemporary writings or excerpts from historical documents which focus on the relationship between God and history or Christianity and culture. It is sent to financial supporters of the Providence Foundation.

Printed in the United States of America
Signature Book Printing
8041 Cessna Ave, Ste 132
Gaithersburg, MD 20879
sbpbooks.com

ISBN: 979-8-218-60545-2

The Bible: Divine or Human?

Evidence of Biblical Infallibility and Support for Building Your Life and Nation on Biblical Truth

Preface

When we read the Bible we are confronted with a claim that requires a response: that is, that this book is the Word of God, the Word of the Almighty One who created and sustains all things. In the Bible God reveals and declares Who He is and how we are to live. We can reject the claim or believe it, but to ignore it is foolish. If it is what it claims to be, the Word of God, then our adherence to its requirements is essential for life, here on the earth and in the eternal hereafter.

Can we know that the claims of the Bible are true? Is there any evidence of its divinity and infallibility? The answer is a resounding YES! The implications of the Bible being the Word of the one and only God are immense.

I have been teaching Biblical worldview for about forty years. In my writings, seminars, presentations, talks, and sermons, I have highlighted how the Bible applies to every area of life, and in particular how it addresses public affairs. I have taught leaders in government, education, business, and the church that the degree to which a person or nation applies God's Word in every area of life, is the degree to which they will be free and prosper. In my recent book, *The Bible: America's Source of Law and Liberty,*[1] I give evidence that our country was founded on and made great by our forefathers' reliance on God and His Holy Word. The Bible has been and is the blueprint for building blessed nations.

A foundational presupposition supporting our transformation teaching is belief in the inerrancy of God's Word — that the Bible is God-breathed; it is inspired. While history affirms that application of Biblical principles produces good fruit in men and nations (this is in fact one support of its divinity), understanding that the Bible is the living Word of the Sovereign

God adds immense weight and life to using it as a blueprint and seeking out its principles on which to build a life and society.

Understanding that the Bible is inerrant is foundational for teaching Biblical worldview. Hence, this booklet presents a brief summary of various proofs that have been given by many people over the centuries. This is not intended to be a systematic theological approach to the subject. There are many good books that explore this subject on such a level.[2] This booklet is rather an inspirational and easy to read, yet thoroughly supported, argument in favor of Biblical inerrancy with the goal of inspiring you to build your life upon the divine precepts in the Bible and also to seek to use them to transform men and nations.

The Bible is the divine, inerrant, inspired, infallible Word of God.

Supernatural Transformation via the Bible

Following the bombing of Pearl Harbor on December 7, 1941, a group of American pilots known as the Doolittle Raiders were sent to bomb Japan. Some of them were shot down, captured, and put in prison, where they suffered greatly. They were given meager food, so little that some slowly starved to death. They were kept in dark, cold, small cells; they were yelled at, beaten, and kicked. Many became diseased and received little care. The anger and hatred toward the guards due to the tortuous conditions consumed many of the prisoners. This went on for two years.

One of the Doolittle Raiders' B-25 bombers taking off from the aircraft carrier USS Hornet, April 18, 1942.

After one prisoner died from starvation, Bob Hite wrote a letter to the prison governor complaining of their intolerable treatment, reminding him it was against all Geneva conference rules. Among other things, he wrote: "If you can't do anything useful, will you please give us the Holy Bible to read?"[3] He had sort of been raised in the church, though really knew little of the faith or the Bible. None of the other captives were true believers, and some were even put off by Christianity.

His letter may have done some good, as afterwards their rations improved and they were allowed to share a few books, one being the Bible. They decided to let each man read the Bible for three weeks before passing it on.

Bob Hite said: "it was the first time that I had ever – I think any of us – the first time any of us had really read the Bible from cover to cover. I was sort of like a man being in the desert and finding a cool pool....Instead of hating this enemy that we had such hate for, we began to feel sorry for them....It was almost a miracle to realize the sort of thing that happened to us...we were no longer afraid to the extent that we had been...we no longer had the hatred."[4]

Just prior to having his turn with the Bible, one of the prisoners, Jake DeShazer, was yelled at by a guard. Rage had been growing within Jake over his two years of imprisonment, so without thought he yelled back. The guard hit him on the head with his fist. Jake kicked him back, with the guard responding by hitting him with his steel scabbard. Jake then threw a bucket of dirty mop water that he had been using to clean the floor on the guard. Oddly the guard only yelled back. "It is strange that he didn't cut off my head," Jake said.[5]

Bob Hite being led to prison by Japanese captors. During his imprisonment Hite was transformed after reading the Bible.

Just after this incident the Bible was passed on to Jake. This experience would turn his life upside-down. He began to read the small print from the dim light coming through the small vent at the top of the cell. "The words of the page came to life. It seemed as though they were written just for him." In the stories he read in the Old Testament and especially in "the story of Christ's suffering in the New, he felt that God was indeed present, reaching out for someone abandoned, as mistreated, as hopeless as he was."[6] In his three weeks with the Bible, he spent every minute reading and memorizing all he could.

"On June 8, 1944, he read for a second time Romans 10:9: 'That if thou shalt confess with thy mouth the Lord Jesus, and shalt believe in thine heart that God hath raised him from the dead, thou shalt be saved.' Jake prayed: 'Lord, though I am far from home and though I am in prison, I must have forgiveness.' As he prayed constantly, thinking deeply about the message of the Bible, he was overcome with a tremendous sensation: 'My heart was filled with joy. I wouldn't have traded places with anyone at that time. Oh, what a great joy it was to know that I was saved, that God had forgiven me my sins….Hunger, starvation, and a freezing cold prison cell no longer had horrors for me. They would only be for a passing moment. Even death could hold no threat when I knew that God had saved me. Death is just one more trial that I must go through before I can enjoy the pleasures of eternal life. There will be no pain, no suffering, no loneliness in heaven. Everything will be perfect with joy forever.'"[7]

The central message of the Scriptures became real and alive to him. In the midst of the worst of conditions, he experienced a supernatural contentment only possible in Christ. There is no worldly explanation for this supernatural transformation. It affirms the divine nature of the Bible.

The more he read the more he realized he needed to change deep down inside. He especially needed Christian love. He felt that while his sins had been forgiven through Christ, he would need to forgive as well. A test soon came his way. One day while returning from exercise, the guard yelled at him to hurry, slapped him, pushed him into his cell and slammed the door on his bare foot breaking some bones. As he sat on the stool, anger beginning to rise, he thought God was testing him somehow in this.

The next morning when the guard was back, he first considered revenge but remembering the lesson, responded by saying "good morning." The guard looked at him strangely since he had never heard Jake say this. Morning after morning Jake tried to be polite and friendly. Finally, the guard came over to him and spoke. Jake asked about his family. This was the beginning of a complete change of treatment from this one guard. From then on the guard treated Jake well, even bringing him food. "I knew then that God's way will work if we really try, no matter what the circumstances."[8]

DeShazer was held captive for about one more year, during which time God did other miracles to keep him alive. After the war, Jacob DeShazer and his wife would serve as missionaries to Japan for 30 years. Through their ministry many Japanese were converted, including two of the guards at his prison, and 23 new churches were started. He also worked closely with Mitsuo Fuchida, who had led the air attack on Pearl Harbor, and after the war became a Christian.[9]

Similar stories to that of Bob Hite and Jacob DeShazer have been repeated hundreds of millions of times since Jesus Christ, the living Word of God, came into the world. The supernatural transformation of men who hear its message shows us that the Bible is powerful. The Bible is unique among all books ever written. It is more than the mere words of men. It is in fact divine. The Bible is God's Word and it is infallible.

Jake DeShazer (right) returned to Japan after the war and led many to Christ, including Mitsuo Fuchida (left) who led the air attack on Pearl Harbor.

Statement of Biblical Inerrancy

God is an eternal perfect being Who created all things, seen and unseen. Man is His highest creation and was made in the very image of God. God knows the physical, moral and spiritual laws that govern His creation. He knows how His creation is to function so as to produce life and blessing. Because of His great love for mankind and His desire to present Truth, He has revealed who He is, His redemptive work through Jesus Christ, and the answers to the basic questions of life through a written revelation, the Bible.[10] He has given mankind a record in human language wherein every word is inspired by God through the men He chose to be co-authors with Him.

Every word, sentence, and book in the Bible is truth and is 100% the Word of God. God chose to use men inspired by the Holy Spirit to write His infallible Word, so the Bible is also 100% by man. Just as Jesus Christ (the Word made flesh, the living Word) is 100% God and 100% man, so also is the Bible 100% by God and 100% by man under the inspiration of the Holy Spirit. Thus, the Bible is divine, inspired, and inerrant as given in the original manuscripts, called the autographs.[11] The mainstream historic church has believed this for two thousand years. This has been the orthodox position of the faithful since the first centuries. Skepticism of Biblical inerrancy only started to develop in the past two centuries and has captured many nominal Christians today, with bad consequences.

If the inerrancy of the Bible is rejected, then all other areas of Christian belief have no permanent foundation upon which to stand. If the Bible is not 100% truth, then all the doctrines that come from the Bible become a matter of man's choice whether to believe them or not. If someone rejects the Bible as God's Word, they can easily reject the death and resurrection of Christ, God's moral standards for living, and any other teaching or command in the Scripture.

The Bible is God's Word, God's thoughts, and God's will for mankind. The Bible is completely true in all that it addresses, and it addresses all spheres of life. The Bible answers the basic questions of life: Who is God? Does He love me? What should I do to please Him? How does He look at my sin? How can I be forgiven? Where will I go when I die? How must I treat others? What is the purpose of life? Why do I exist? No other religion or ideology can answer these sufficiently.

God's Word does not stop here, but it instructs us in everyday life, from family matters to economic and civil affairs. Some of those areas addressed by the Bible include: worship, personal conduct, family, child raising, value of man, character in society, societal structure, health and sanitation, work

The Bible: Divine or Human?   7

and rest, social needs and justice, government and law, economics, business, liberty, education, crime and punishment, warfare, philosophy, arts and media, science and technology, history and literature.[12] The Bible is the standard by which we are to measure all areas of life and thought. To the degree that we do so, and then live in accordance with God's truth, things will go well for us and our society.

Before we explore the evidence, please note that belief in Biblical inerrancy does not mean that everything recorded in the Bible is a statement of something true. For example, the advice of Job's friends was not true and right advice, but the words recorded in the book of Job are the true words of those people. Biblical inerrancy also does not mean that every verse of Scripture must be interpreted literally. There are many passages in the Bible that are not intended to be taken literally, for example: Jesus saying, "I am the door," the visions of various prophets, and much of the book of Revelation. In addition to believing the Bible is inerrant, we must also correctly interpret the Bible; that is, we must have correct hermeneutics. There are many people who believe in Biblical inerrancy but have bad theological ideas. We need to believe in Biblical inspiration and also learn how to correctly understand what God is saying in His inspired Word.

Historical View of Inerrancy

Many people throughout history have testified of the Bible's value and of its divine nature. Significant church fathers and historic creeds declared the inerrancy of the Bible. Clement of Rome (died 99 A.D.) wrote in the first century: "Look carefully into the Scriptures, which are the true utterances of the Holy Spirit. Observe that nothing of an unjust or counterfeit character is written in them."[13] A century later church theologian Irenaeus (130-202 A.D.) concluded, "The Scriptures are indeed perfect, since they were spoken by the Word of God and his Spirit."[14]

Prolific Christian writer, Tertullian (c. 155- c. 240) said, "The statements of Holy Scripture will never be discordant with truth."[15] Bishop of North Africa and influential Christian theologian, Augustine (354-430) wrote, "I have learned to yield this [total] respect and honor only to the canonical books of Scripture. Of these alone do I most

Augustine of Hippo believed the Biblical writers "were completely free from error."

firmly believe that their authors were completely free from error."[16]

The Nicene Creed (325 A.D.) states: "We believe ... the Holy Spirit ... has spoken through the prophets."[17] The Lutheran Apology of the Augsburg Confession identifies Holy Scripture with the Word of God and calls the Holy Spirit the author of the Bible. Because of this, Lutherans confess in the Formula of Concord, "We receive and embrace with our whole heart the prophetic and apostolic Scriptures of the Old and New Testaments as the pure, clear fountain of Israel."[18]

The Nicene Creed, like most historic creeds of the church, embraced the divinity of the Bible.

The Scots Confession (1560) states: "As we believe and confess the Scriptures of God sufficient to instruct and make perfect the man of God, so do we affirm and avow their authority to be from God, and not to depend on men or angels."[19] The Second Helvetic Confessions (reflecting Swiss-German Reformed Protestantism, from 1560s) says: "We believe and confess the canonical Scriptures of the holy prophets and apostles of both Testaments to be the true Word of God, and to have sufficient authority of themselves, not of men. For God himself spoke to the fathers, prophets, apostles, and still speaks to us through the Holy Scriptures."[20]

The Presbyterian Confession of Faith, first adopted in the seventeenth century, clearly states its belief in the infallibility and inerrancy of Scripture. The view of this document is summarized in *A Brief Statement of Belief, II*: "The Scriptures of the Old and New Testaments, written by men inspired by the Holy Spirit, are the word of God. They are the revelation of God's will for man and of man's duty to God, and are the only infallible and authoritative rule of faith and life."[21] The Westminster Larger Catechism states that "the holy Scriptures of the Old and New Testament are the word of God, the only rule of faith and obedience."[22]

The leaders of the Protestant Reformation, such as Martin Luther, John Calvin, William Tyndale, and John Knox held to Biblical inerrancy and worked to get copies of the Scriptures into the common languages of the people.[23] Orthodox Christians have embraced this view up until the present, though many liberal critics have attacked it in more recent times. A modern council of church leaders expanded on this idea in *The Chicago Statement on Biblical Inerrancy* (1978). In part it states: "Holy Scripture, being God's

The Bible: Divine or Human?

own Word, written by men prepared and superintended by His Spirit, is of infallible divine authority in all matters upon which it touches: it is to be believed, as God's instruction, in all that it affirms; obeyed, as God's command, in all that it requires; embraced, as God's pledge, in all that it promises."[24]

It was not only church leaders who believed in Biblical infallibility. Consider the great European political philosopher John Locke who said: "The holy Scripture is to me, and always will be, the constant guide of my assent; and I shall always hearken to it, as containing infallible truth....Where I want the evidence of things, there yet is ground enough for me to believe, because God has said it."[25]

Political philosopher John Locke believed Scripture was infallible truth.

English jurist William Blackstone believed the Bible revealed the will of God and His divine law, writing in his *Commentaries on the Laws of England*:

> This will of his maker is called the law of nature....This law of nature, being co-eval with mankind and dictated by God himself, is of course superior in obligation to any other. It is binding over all the globe, in all countries, and at all times: no human laws are of any validity, if contrary to this; and such of them as are valid derive all their force, and all their authority, mediately or immediately, from this original....
>
> The doctrines thus delivered we call the revealed or divine law, and they are to be found only in the holy scriptures. These precepts, when revealed, are found upon comparison to be really a part of the original law of nature....As then the moral precepts of this law are indeed of the same original with those of the law of nature....the revealed law...is the law of nature expressly declared to be so by God himself....Upon these two foundations, the law of nature and the law of revelation, depend all human laws; that is to say, no human laws should be suffered to contradict these.[26]

Divine Nature of the Bible in American History

America was built upon the Bible. A large majority of the Founding Fathers believed in the divinity of the Scriptures, which is reflected in their words, their laws and constitutions, their motives for starting schools and colleges, and their actions.[27]

The divine nature of the Bible was a fundamental tenet of almost every (if not every) denomination and church in early America, as evidenced by their catechisms. Christian catechisms were not only used in churches but also in schools and textbooks, such as the New England Primer. Even early Unitarianism "strictly adhered to the great Protestant principle, 'the Bible – the Bible only,'" as the source of their faith beliefs.[28]

The first settlers believed the Bible was infallible and inspired. The Governor of the Plymouth Colony, William Bradford, wrote: "The honour of infallibility…belongs only to the word of God and the pure testament of Christ, to be followed as the only rule and pattern for direction by all Churches and Christians."[29] Since the New England Pilgrims and Puritans viewed the Bible as the inerrant Word of God and the supreme authority in all of life, it served as the source of their civil laws. The Plymouth Colonies' *Book of General Laws* (1671) begins by stating that "Laws…are so far good and wholesome, as by how much they are derived from, and agreeable to the ancient Platform of Gods Law."[30]

The first American constitution was written by Rev. Thomas Hooker in 1638. The oath imposed on the magistrates bound them "to administer justice according to the laws here established, and for want thereof according to the rule of the word of God."[31] Established in 1638 under the guidance of Rev. John Davenport, the New Haven Colony rested its frame of government upon the idea that "the Scriptures doe holde forth a perfect rule for the direction and government of all men in all duet[ies]…in the government of famyles and commonwealths."[32]

Statue of Governor William Bradford in Plymouth, Massachusetts. He, like most early civil leaders, believed the Bible was infallible and is why they based their civil laws upon its truth.

The Pentateuch (the first five books of the Bible) was the basis for the criminal code of the Massachusetts Body of Liberties, written in 1641 by Rev. Nathaniel Ward. If situations arose not addressed by the Body of Liberties, it states: "in case of the defect of a law in any case" the standard was "the word of God."[33]

To these early Americans, the Bible presented the perfect rule because they believed it to be perfect, inerrant, and inspired. In fact, you had to believe this to hold public office in many of the colonies and states. The Constitution of Delaware (1776) required government officials to take the following oath of office before assuming duties: "I, A.B. do profess faith in

God the Father and in Jesus Christ His only Son, and in the Holy Ghost, one God blessed for evermore; and I do acknowledge the Holy Scriptures of the Old and New Testament to be given by Divine inspiration."[34]

The Frame of Government of Pennsylvania, 1776, required that "each member, before he takes his seat, shall make and subscribe the following declaration, viz: 'I do believe in one God, the creator and governor of the universe, the rewarder of the good and the punisher of the wicked. And I do acknowledge the Scriptures of the Old and New Testament to be given by Divine inspiration.'"[35]

The Bible was the bedrock upon which America rested. It has always been greatly venerated and believed to be the Word of God. In recent years as secularism has increased, the Bible has become to be viewed by an increasing number of Americans as just another book. In 1963, 65 percent of Americans believed the Bible was infallible. By 1982 that number had fallen to 37 percent.[36] Nonetheless, it still retains a very significant place in the thinking of most Americans. A survey from 2014 reveals that 79% of Americans strongly or somewhat agree that "following the Bible's teachings would be good for American society."[37]

Recent studies by the Barna Group reveal the important but diminishing view of the Bible among Americans. Three out four people age 70 and above believe the Bible to be authoritative. That percentage gradually decreases with each younger age group to where among the youngest generation of Americans (Millennials, age 18 to 31) fewer than half believe the Bible is authoritative.[38] However, believing the Bible is authoritative is not the same as believing it is infallible. Rejecting the inerrancy of the Bible leads to the individual as the one who determines what precepts and standards they will obey. Both a decline in seeing the Bible as special and a casting aside of belief in Biblical inerrancy has led to the decline of the nation. Presenting evidence such as is in this book will help to change this downward trend.

The Words of the Founders

The men who gave birth to the American republic were primarily Christians who embraced a belief in the divinity of the Bible. Consider the words of a few of them. John Jay, First Chief Justice of the U.S. Supreme Court wrote: "The Bible is the best of all books, for it is the word of God and teaches us the way to be happy in this world and in the next. Continue therefore to read it and to

First Chief Justice John Jay wrote, "the Bible…is the word of God."

John Quincy Adams

regulate your life by its precepts."[39] President John Quincy Adams stated: "Let us, then, search the Scriptures....The Bible contains the revelation of the will of God. It contains the history of the creation of the world, and of mankind."[40]

To the Founders, the Bible was the means to know God and His purpose for life. As President of Columbia College in New York, William Johnson, a signer of the U.S. Constitution, gave a commencement speech where he reminded the graduates that the purpose of their education was "to qualify you the better to serve your Creator and your country....Your first great duties...are those you owe to Heaven, to your Creator and Redeemer.... Remember, too, that you are the redeemed of the Lord, that you are bought with a price, even the inestimable price of the precious blood of the Son of God.... Love, fear, and serve Him as your Creator, Redeemer, and Sanctifier. Acquaint yourselves with Him in His Word and holy ordinances. Make Him your friend and protector and your felicity is secured both here and hereafter."[41]

Signer of the Declaration Robert Treat Paine said: "I believe the Bible to be the written word of God & to contain in it the whole rule of faith & manners."[42] Roger Sherman, Signer of the Declaration and the U.S. Constitution wrote:

> I believe that there is one only living and true God, existing in three persons, the Father, the Son, and the Holy Ghost, the same in substance equal in power and glory. That the scriptures of the old and new testaments are a revelation from God and a complete rule to direct us how we may glorify and enjoy Him.[43]

Author of the first exhaustive English dictionary, Noah Webster, believed the source of all truth was the Bible:

Roger Sherman believed the Scriptures "are a revelation from God."

> As the will of God is our rule of action, and that will can be fully known only from revelation, the Bible must be considered as the great source of all the truths by which men are to be guided in government, as well as in all social

transactions…. the Bible [is] the instrument of all reformation in morals and religion.[44]

When Thomas Paine published a tract arguing that the Bible was not the Word of God, Patrick Henry, who believed that "the Bible is worth all the books that ever were printed,"[45] wrote a rebuttal giving proof that it was. Before this could be published he was given Bishop Richard Watson's *Apology for the Bible*, which Henry said answered all of Paine's arguments so well that his work was not necessary.[46]

Education

Schools were started in colonial America to teach people how to read the Bible. Colleges were started to train ministers to become knowledgeable of the Scriptures. Early textbooks contained catechisms that taught the inspiration of the Scripture.[47] Civics books presented the view that law is rooted in Divine revelation. Andrew Young's *First Lessons in Civil Government* (1846) states:

The Regulations of Yale College in 1745:"1. All scholars shall live religious, godly, and blameless lives according to the rules of God's Word, diligently reading the Holy Scriptures, the fountain of light and truth."

> The will of the Creator is the law of nature which men are bound to obey. But mankind in their present imperfect state are not capable of discovering in all cases what the law of nature requires; it has therefore pleased Divine Providence to reveal his will to mankind, to instruct them in their duties to himself and to each other. This will is revealed in the Holy Scriptures, and is called the law of revelation, or the Divine law.[48]

The Founders Started Numerous Bible Societies.

Believing in the divinity and value of Scripture motivated early Americans to start numerous organizations to circulate the Bible. Many of our Founding Fathers were greatly involved in these Bible societies, including:

- John Marshall (Supreme Court Chief Justice), Vice-president of the American Bible Society
- James McHenry (Signer of Constitution), President of the Baltimore Bible Society

- John Langdon (Signer of Constitution), VP of the American Bible Society
- Rufus King (Signer of Constitution), Member of New York Bible Society
- John Quincy Adams, VP of the American Bible Society
- Elias Boudinot (President of the Continental Congress), Founder and first President of the American Bible Society, President of the New Jersey Bible Society
- Caleb Strong (Constitutional Convention), VP of the American Bible Society
- John Jay (Original Chief Justice of the US Supreme Court), President of the American Bible Society
- Charles Cotesworth Pinckney (Signer of Constitution), President of the Charleston Bible Society, VP of the American Bible Society
- Rufus Putnam (General in American Revolution, Federal Judge), President of the Ohio Bible Society
- Benjamin Rush (Signer of Declaration), Founder and manager of the Philadelphia Bible Society
- Bushrod Washington (US Supreme Court Justice), VP of the American Bible Society

Bible on which George Washington took the presidential oath, 1789.

In 1816 sixty delegates representing 35 of these local societies gathered in New York City and formed the American Bible Society. During the first year 85 local societies joined with it. Elias Boudinot became the first president. Boudinot had been a member of the Continental Congress, chosen as president in 1782 and in that capacity a signer of the Treaty of Peace officially ending the war, a member of the first House of Representatives (1789-1796), and the Director of the National Mint (1796-1805). In accepting the office of President of the American Bible Society, Boudinot wrote: "I am not ashamed to confess that I accept the appointment of President of the American Bible Society as the greatest honor that could have been conferred on me this side of the grave."[49] He continued as president of the society until his death in 1821. The first Supreme Court Chief Justice, John Jay, served as President of the American Bible Society as well. General Rufus Putnam founded the first Bible society west of the Alleghenies.

Reasons the Bible Is the Word of God

Biblical inerrancy has been a part of orthodox belief throughout the Christian era. True Christians have been "people of the Book." Why does (or should) the Christian accept the Bible as the foundation of his life and worldview? It is because the Bible is the Word of God — the Word of the infinite, eternal, almighty, omniscient Creator. It is perfect and true, and reveals the nature and character of God and the standard of all that is right in the universe. If we do not believe or do not obey the Bible, we are disbelieving and disobeying God.

Does the Christian just accept the divinity of the Bible on blind faith? Is there any evidence for the Bible being the Word of God? No, we don't accept this on blind faith, and yes, there is an abundance of evidence for us to believe that the Bible is God's Word!

So, how do we know that the Bible is God's word? Before answering this let's first briefly look at the Book as a whole.

The Bible is more than just a holy book. It is a book from God about God. Its story is about God's love for man and His plan for man's redemption. It contains "the revelations of God, the principles of Christian faith, and the rules of practice."[50] It reveals how man should live in order to experience the great blessing of God. Furthermore, it presents God's purpose for man as well as God's larger purpose to restore all things as He intended from the beginning.

Its central figure is Jesus Christ, God robed in humanity, and it presents a record of His origin, birth, life, death, and resurrection. Its message is stranger than fiction because it tells us about the God who made the universe and everything in it, including our planet earth, and then visited it to provide a way for man to get to heaven and to show man how he may share in God's kingdom and be a part of His family.

The Bible is not just a history book, although it is accurate in all the history it presents. It is not merely a book of literature and poetry, although is has inspired many songs and great writings. It is not just an adventure story, although it contains some of the most dramatic events ever. It is not merely a book of ethics or morality, although the best laws have come from its principles. It is not a text book of natural history, although it contains no contradiction to science.

"The Bible is a unique record of man's problem and God's own answer, the Good News of salvation from sin through Jesus."[51] It is a blueprint for how to please the Creator and establish His Kingdom on earth as it is in heaven. Other books may become dated and their usefulness exhausted, but the Bible is always up-to-date and its message always pertinent. Its depth of knowledge can never be mined. The more we study it the more we discover its great truths.

Mark Twain said: "It's not the things I don't understand in the Bible that bother me; it's the things I do understand!"[52] This is why many people are afraid to study it; they may meet the Author and they are not ready to act upon the consequences of doing so.

The Bible Claims It Is the Word of God.

The Bible frequently claims that the words of Scripture are God's words. There is never any attempt to prove this. It is stated as fact. For example:

- "Thus says the Lord" — used hundreds of times in the Old Testament.
- "God said" — used 9 times in the first chapter of Genesis, and myriads more times in other places.
- "Saith the Lord" — 23 times in the book of Malachi, and throughout the Bible.
- "The Lord spoke" — 560 times in the first five books of the Bible.
- The prophets claimed numerous times that their words were the words of God (Isaiah, over 40 times; Jeremiah over 100 times, etc.). When they wrote "Thus says the Lord," they were claiming that their words were the words of the Sovereign God, and as such they were authoritative. Their words had to come from God and prove true or they would be a false prophet, subject to being put to death (Num. 22:38; Deut. 18:18-20; Jer. 1:9; 14:14; 23:16-22; 29:31-21; Ezek. 2:7; 13:1-16). In addition, God is often said to speak through the prophet, hence, God's words were the prophet's words (1 Kings 14:18; 16:12, 34; Jer. 37:2; Zech 7:7).
- New Testament writers claimed their message was from God; for example, Paul says in 1 Cor. 14:37 "that what I am writing to you is a command of the Lord."
- Jesus quoted from at least 24 Old Testament books. In Luke 24: 24-27, He claimed Himself to be the subject of prophecy all through the Old Testament. He said Scripture must be fulfilled (Matt. 13:14; Luke 21:22, John 13:18). He claimed His own words were inspired (Mark 13:31, John 6:63). In John 10:35 He said Scripture cannot be broken. His own claims to Divine origin and the claims of the Bible stand or fall together.[53] If He cannot be proved a liar or a lunatic, the Bible is God's Word.[54]

- New Testament passages also indicate that the Old Testament was the inspired word of God. 2 Tim. 3:16 states that all of the Old Testament writings are God's words. — "All Scripture is given by inspiration of God [lit., God-breathed] and is profitable for doctrine, for reproof, for correction, for instruction in righteousness." God breathed it out. It is directly from God's mouth. Men wrote, but He directed what they would write. In this passage "Scripture" (Greek, *graphē*) certainly refers to all the Old Testament because that is what the word *graphē* refers to in all of its 51 occurrences in the New Testament.[55] Other passages from the New Testament supporting the Old Testament as God's words include Luke 24:25, 27, 44; Acts 3:18; 24:14; Rom. 15:4.

Jesus declared that the Word of God is truth.

- There are numerous New Testament passages that speak of specific parts of the Old Testament as God's words. These include: In Matthew 1:22, Isaiah's words from Isa. 7:14 were referred to as "that what was spoken by the Lord through the prophet." In Matthew 4:4 Jesus said that man should live by "every word that proceeds out of the mouth of God" and He uses many Old Testament Scriptures as that food from God's mouth to combat Satan and his temptations. A few others examples include Matthew 19:5, Mark 7:9-13, Acts 1:16, and Acts 2:16-17.
- Peter writes that no prophecy in Scripture came "by an act of human will" ["by the impulse of man"] but by "men moved by the Holy Spirit spoke from God" (2 Peter 1:20-21).
- "Jesus and the New Testament authors quote various parts of the Old Testament Scriptures as divinely authoritative over 295 times."[56]

Scripture claims it is divine in origin over 3800 times. It was given by divine inspiration (2 Pet. 1:20-21); it was breathed out by God (2 Tim. 3:16). Every word in the Bible is the word that God spoke (and still speaks today), though he used human agents to write these words down.

Inspiration is that divine influence of the Holy Spirit upon the writers of Scripture whereby their writings are made infallible. The Scriptures are infallible. While the men were fallible, God worked in such a way that those fallible men produced God's infallible Word. Man is not of primary importance in inspiration; rather, the Holy Spirit is. Scripture is infallible because God breathed it. Man was not just inspired to write and then God sanctified it, but God moved in such a way that it is infallible. Every word is important.

Revelation is God making Himself and His will known to man. Inspiration is the record of God's revelation. Men today need **illumination**. They need enlightenment to understand the truth that God revealed and inspired men to record. The Holy Spirit is the source of illumination, just as He was the source of inspiration.

The primary reason for belief in the Bible as the Word of God is divine illumination.

Regenerated believers full of the Holy Spirit will be convinced of the Bible's claims to be God's Words as they read the Bible. The more Christians read the Bible, the more they are convinced of its divinity "from the inward work of the Holy Spirit bearing witness by and with the Word in our hearts."[57] This is the highest source of appeal to attest to the divine claims of Scripture. There is no higher appeal than to God. "The natural man does not receive the things of the Spirit of God, for they are folly to him, and he is not able to understand them because they are spiritually discerned" (1 Cor. 2:14). The Scriptures are *self-attesting*, both in stating their divinity and in affirming in our hearts and minds via the Holy Spirit their divine nature.[58]

To the unenlightened who read it, the Bible is an amazing book, containing the best ideas on all kinds of subjects. For example, to Thomas Jefferson the Bible contained the best moral teachings in the world. However, to the believer it is much more. It is the Word of almighty God, and is full of power and life. **It is strangely alive**, as the Bible translator J.B. Phillips said. God's sheep hear His voice (John 10:27), so when we read the Bible, we hear His voice. We have an assurance this is the Word of God, unlike nonbelievers who do not and cannot have such assurance. (The Bible is God's Word regardless if it is accepted as such by unbelievers. Personal belief does not make it so. However, the conscious reality of its divine nature by the regenerate causes it to be of immense more value and is approached in a much different way. Such a view of the Bible by most of the Founders of America is why they sought to build the nation upon its precepts.)

Question 4 of the Westminster Larger Catechism gives the primary reason that the Bible is the Word of God: "The Scriptures manifest themselves to be the word of God, by their majesty and purity; by the consent of all the parts, and the scope of the whole, which is to give all glory to God; by their light and power to convince and convert sinners, to comfort and build up believers unto salvation. But the Spirit of God bearing witness by and with the Scriptures in the heart of man, is alone able fully to persuade it that they are the very word of God." (John 16:13-14; 1 Cor. 2:6-9)

Self-attestation, while primary, is not the only reason to believe the Bible is God's Word. Seven other sources of evidence for the divine inspiration of the Bible are presented below.

Evidences of Biblical Inspiration

1. The Bible's Survival[59]

From its beginning, the Bible has survived ongoing attempts to destroy it.[60] Likewise, those people that follow its teachings have survived centuries of persecution. Men have been killed for owning copies of the Bible in each century, and they are still being killed today. Their persecution has been recorded in such works as *Foxe's Book of Martyrs, Fair Sunshine*, and *By Their Blood*.[61]

No ancient book has close to as many surviving copies. While the classics of Plato, Herodotus, and others have from one to 20 manuscripts, there are over 5600 portions of Old and New Testament manuscripts dating from a few centuries before Christ and following,[62] with only minor and insignificant variations. Recognition of the divine nature of the Bible caused its adherents to take great care in copying the manuscripts.

Scottish covenanter and martyr, James Renwick, on the gallows. In each century of the Christian era people have been put to death for seeking to read the Bible and live according to its ideas.

From the time the first books of the Old Testament were written in the middle of the second millennium before Christ up until Johann Gutenberg invented the moveable type printing press around 1455 AD, all copies of the Scriptures were done by hand. For centuries prior to the press, the job of scribes was to painstakingly copy Scripture. Such care was taken that some of them would use a new pen every time they came to the word *Lord*, and then they would reread what had been copied to assure its accuracy. Since Lord is used 7736 times in the Bible, they changed pens and checked their work a great deal!

John Wycliffe translated the Bible into English because he wanted the Scripture to become the common property of all.

Prior to and during the Protestant Reformation there was a flourish of new Bible translations. Beginning with John Wycliffe in the late 14th century and in the centuries that followed, many men began to translate the Bible into the common language of the people. Many religious and civil authorities sought to stop this effort, persecuting and killing many of the translators as well as those who read the Book.

Yet, in spite of all the attempts to wipe out the Bible, it not only survived but flourished. It is by far the most widely printed book in history, totaling 5-6 billion copies, and it is the annual bestseller at 100 million per year. It is available to more people and in more languages than any book: 98% of the world's population has access to parts of or the whole Bible. The New Testament is currently translated into 1185 languages, and translations are in progress for 1300 other languages.[63]

While many attempts have been made to stamp out the Bible, this will never happen, as history has shown. Why is this? It is because the Bible is God's Word to man. It is the Creator's revelation to us of who He is, why He created us, and how we are to live. He will not allow His Word to be removed from the world because we need it to accomplish our purpose and mission for Him.

The French Enlightenment writer Voltaire said: "In one hundred years, this book will be forgotten." Today, Voltaire is forgotten and more Bibles are being printed and sold than ever before. One hundred years after his boast, his house was being used as the headquarters for the Geneva Bible Society.[64]

Jesus affirmed the permanent nature of God's Word, declaring, "Heaven and earth will pass away, but My words shall not pass away" (Matt. 24:35). He said, "It is easier for heaven and earth to pass away than for one stroke of a letter of the Law to fail" (Luke 16:17). God has magnified His Word above His name (Ps. 138:2).

God's Word, the Bible, will remain because it is alive. The book of Hebrews states, "For the word of God is living and active and sharper than any two-edged sword, and piercing as far as the division of soul and spirit, of both joints and marrow, and able to judge the thoughts and intentions of the heart" (Heb. 4:12). The words that God speaks are sharp: "But when they heard this, they were cut to the quick and were intending to slay them" (Acts 5:33). His Word will accomplish what He sends it to do (Isa. 55:11).

2. The Bible's Structure and Internal Consistency

The Bible is unique in its message, its form, and in how it was written. It is comprised of 66 individual books, 39 in the Old Testament and 27 in the New Testament. It was written by dozens of different people from a variety of professions and social standings, in a variety of literary styles, over many centuries, in three languages, on three continents. It also addresses myriads of controversial subjects, such as marriage and divorce, homosexuality, obedience to authority, use of force, parenting, and the nature of God. It is not short: the King James Version has 1189 chapters, 31,173 verses, and 773,692 words.

In spite of its great diversity, the Bible presents a unified message throughout its entirety. It tells the story of man's redemption through God's mercy and intimate involvement in His creation. All the while it is consistent in its moral precepts and philosophical worldview. A just and loving God underlies all the lessons and history from Genesis to Revelation. His nature, attributes, and divine power are consistent throughout the divine Book. In addition, its messages have been proven through history and practice to work. Most importantly, the central character seen throughout the entire Bible is the most amazing figure in all of history. That figure is the God-man Jesus Christ. The one, true, living God made known through Jesus Christ is revealed to mankind throughout the pages of the Bible. He is not only presented as the King of all creation, but also as the savior and friend of those who believe in Him.

To understand the Bible's unique and diverse origination, consider this analogy. Imagine you are sitting in a room and you witness a man come in carrying an odd marble shape that he had chiseled, which he places on the floor and leaves. Over time about forty different men do the same thing adding to the original structure unique marble pieces that they have prepared. After the last man places his piece with the others, you see a beautiful statue. Then you learn that most of these men were strangers and from many different locations. You would conclude that one mind planned this and sent to each man accurate specifications for his piece of marble. The writing of the Bible is like this, with God as the master planner. Peter writes: "For no prophecy was ever made by an act of human will, but men moved by the Holy Spirit spoke from God" (2 Pet. 1:21).

Take 40 different people from every walk of life – including doctors, shepherds, kings, religious leaders, tax collectors, military leaders, and fishermen – over a 1500 year period, who live miles and generations apart. Ask them to write on history, law, religion, government, poetry, education, health, ethics, science, morality, and philosophy. Ask them to make predictions of future events, to give guidelines for structuring free and prosperous societies, to write on the meaning of life, and to expound on man's earthly and final purpose. Then you be the editor, and collect, condense, and divide the writings into books.[65] What do you get? A jumbled mass of unrelated, disjointed, and contrary ideas. Yet, the Bible was written just like this, and its message is one amazing whole from Genesis to Revelation. It is united in theme, consistent in concept, logical, and agreed in doctrine.[66] Its great diversity, while maintaining its unity, affirms the Bible's divine origin.

3. The Bible's Scientific and Historic Accuracy

"The God of the Bible is the God Who created the universe."[67] He created the physical (as well as moral) laws by which it operates. "True science and Scripture will always agree — they both have the same Author."[68] Opinions of science have differed from the Bible, but no scientific inaccuracy has been recorded in the Scripture. Its statements are true under the closest tests.

The Father of Oceanography and the man who first discovered and charted the ocean currents, Matthew Fontaine Maury, wrote that "the Bible and science do not conflict if each is rightly interpreted."[69] Maury, like a majority of the leading scientists in history, believed the Bible was the Word of God and conducted his significant work in the context of a Biblical worldview. He said:

> I have been blamed by men of science, both in this country and in England, for quoting the Bible in confirmation of the doctrines of physical geography. The Bible, they say, was not written for scientific purposes, and is therefore of no authority in matters of science. I beg pardon! The Bible is authority for everything it touches....The Bible is true and science is true. The agents concerned in the physical economy of our planet are ministers of His who made both it and the Bible. The records which He has chosen to make through the agency of these ministers of His upon the crust of the earth are as true as the records which, by the hands of His prophets and servants, He has been pleased to make in the Book of Life. They are both true; and

when your men of science, with vain and hasty conceit, announce the discovery of disagreement between them, rely upon it the fault is not with the Witness or His records, but with the "worm" who essays to interpret evidence which he does not understand.[70]

History affirms that science has never developed significantly anywhere except where there was a Christian influence; that is, in western civilization, which has its roots in Christianity. The scientific method and motivation for enquiry stems from Scriptural concepts — that the universe is the orderly product of a Divine Mind, and that man can discover the secrets of His creation, since he is made in His image.[71] Such ideas are not naturally a product of eastern thought, which is random and chaotic, and explains the lack of scientific development in nations where eastern philosophies have been dominant.

Most of the great scientists knew the Bible and its Author, including Isaac Newton, Johann Kepler, William Herschel, James Maxwell, Francis Bacon, Carolus Linneaus, Blaise Pascal, James Joule, Michael Faraday, John Herschel, Robert Boyle, Louis Agazziz, and Lord Kelvin. These men believed that there is no contradiction in what the Bible teaches and what we see in creation.

While not a science book, the Bible gives much scientific insight, even long before man discovered such things, including:

- Spherical nature of the earth (Is. 40:21-22; Pr. 8:27; Job 26:10)
- Free floating of the earth in space (Job 26:7 — "He hangs the earth on nothing.")
- Moon is a reflector (Job 25:5)
- Life is in the blood (Lev. 7:11) — man discovered this about 300 years ago; the Bible said it over 3500 years ago.
- Circulation of the atmosphere (Eccl. 1:6)

Isaac Newton wrote: "We are to... acknowledge one God, infinite, eternal, omnipresent, omniscient, omnipotent, the Creator of all things, most wise, most just, most good, most holy. We must love him...obey his commandments, and set times apart for his service...for this is the love of God that we keep his commandments, and his commandments are not grievous (I John 5:3)." - *Philosophy of Nature*

- Sanitation – cover excrement to prohibit spread of germs (Deut. 23:9-24). Man did not discover germs until the mid 19th century.
- Cleanliness – cleansing after contact with those who have died (Num. 19:11-22)
- Quarantine to stop the spread of infectious diseases (Deut. 24:4; Lev. 13-15)
- Pathways in the oceans (Ps. 8:8)

Matthew Maury was originally inspired to find the ocean currents when Scripture was read to him. A monument honoring Maury was dedicated in Richmond, Virginia, in 1929. A writer for the Richmond Times, Virginia Lee Cox, spoke of this Biblical inspiration in describing the monument in a newspaper article of the day. Cox wrote:

Maury statue with the Bible at the base.

On the plinth of the monument in the flattest relief are figures of fish, representing Maury's interest in the paths of the sea. The story goes that once when Maury was ill he had his son read the Bible to him each night. One night he read the eighth Psalm, and when he came to the passage — "The fishes of the sea and whatsoever walketh through the paths of the sea" — Maury had him read it over several times. Finally he said, "If God says there are paths in the sea I am going to find them if I get out of this bed." Thus the Psalm was the direct inspiration for his discoveries….

In his right hand are the pencil and the compass, and in his left hand a chart. Against his chair is the Bible, from which he drew inspiration for his explorations. The sculptor has caught amazingly the spirit of the man.[72]

The study of science is important for many reasons. Foremost, we are to search out what God has hidden in His creation so we can more effectively take dominion over the earth and fulfill His purposes. James Maxwell (1831-1879), Scottish physicist and mathematician, reflected in his following prayer the proper view scientists should have when they approach the study of the universe from God's perspective:

> Almighty God, Who has created man in Thine own image, and made him a living soul that he might seek after Thee, and have dominion over Thy creatures, teach us to study the works of Thy hands, that we may subdue the earth to our use, and strengthen the reason for Thy service.[73]

While important, science is limited in what it can do. Science cannot tell where the universe came from nor the reason for which the universe exists. Science "can tell what we are able to do, but not what we ought to do."[74] For this we need the revelation of the Bible.

Psalm 19 tells us that God reveals Himself in science in a general way, and reveals Himself in the Bible in a specific way. Verses 1-6 speak of general revelation, the gospel in the sky (or creation). Verses 7-10 present special revelation, the gospel in the book (the Bible). Verses 11-14 speak of getting His liberating gospel in our hearts, so that we act upon His words and gain "great reward" (v. 11). God's revelation in science shows His power (Ps. 8:3-6). God's revelation in Scripture shows His purpose (Ps. 19:7-14).

The Bible has not only been proven to be scientifically accurate, it has also been proven to be historically accurate. After all, history is His story, and He is the one directing events in time to fulfill His purposes. In years past, skeptics have attacked the Bible claiming much of its history is not true. Yet, new archaeological discoveries have time and time again confirmed that the men and events presented in the Bible are real and accurate. Much has been written on the vast archaeological support of the historical authenticity of the Bible.[75]

4. The Bible's Prophetic Proclamations and Fulfillment

The Bible, as no other book, dares to accurately predict the future. "God arranges the situations of history to bring about His glory in the lives of those who respond to His call"[76] and to bring about His plan for mankind on the earth.

There are about 4000 verses in Scripture (about one in 8) that are prophetic — they tell of future events. The Lord says: "For I the Lord shall speak, and whatever word I speak will be performed" (Ezek. 12:25). Buddhists, Muslims, and followers of Confucius have writings, but the element of prophecy is missing.

Biblical prophecies are not vague and general, like Nostradamus (you may remember that his vague prophecies came up when the Twin Towers fell), but many are very precise. Consider the example of the city of Tyre.

Tyre was a wealthy center of commerce, but because of its sin, God announced its destruction through the prophet Ezekiel (written about 590 BC). Ezekiel 26:7-11 forecasts Nebuchadnezzar's attack on the city. This occurred not long afterward in exact accord with the words of the prophet. However, new Tyre, built on an island half a mile off shore, remained standing. Ezekiel 26:3-5, 12-14 contained improbable details that seemed unlikely to be fulfilled:

> "Thus says the Lord God, 'Behold, I am against you, O Tyre, and I will bring up many nations against you...and they will destroy the walls of Tyre and break down her towers; and I will scrape her debris from her and make her a bare rock. She will be a place for the spreading of nets in the midst of the sea....They will...break down your walls and destroy your pleasant homes, and throw your stones and your timbers and your debris into the water....You will be a place for the spreading of nets. You will be built no more."

Over 250 years later in 332 BC, many nations (vs. 3), under Alexander the Great, came against Tyre. The Tyrians felt safe, but Alexander took the stones and timber of the ruined buildings on the mainland and used them to build a causeway to the island, scraping the very dust of the city to do it. The site of the original city became an unimportant place where fishermen lived, and has long been a barren, flat place for the spreading of nets (vs. 4, 5, 12).

Another prominent example of fulfilled prophecy is the prediction of the fall of Babylon. This city was initially built by men for the glory of men in disobedience to God's command to spread out and fill the earth (see Genesis 10:8-12; 11:1-9). God thwarted this attempt by man to set up a secular civilization by confusing the language of those at Babel, which led to the scattering of these people throughout the earth (Genesis 11:8-9). But worldly people do not give up easily, and so at a later time under the leadership of King Nebuchadnezzar the city of Babylon was re-founded and built into the mightiest city on earth. It was this empire that eventually destroyed Jerusalem in 586 B.C. and carried many into exile, including Daniel.

Babylon was a truly "golden" city. (Nebuchadnezzar, who represented the city, was depicted as a gold head in the dream God gave to the King [see Daniel 2].) It was called "the beauty of kingdoms, the glory of the Chaldean's pride" (Is. 13:19). The walls that surrounded the city were 60 miles in circumference, 300 feet high, and at places 75 feet wide. A moat surrounded the walls and there were 25 brazen gates in each of the four sides. Inside the city was Nebuchadnezzar's palace which was enclosed by walls six miles in circumference. This contained the famous "hanging gardens" which were sustained by arches upon arches, mounding up to 400 feet in height. Babylon was known for learning, for skill in many arts, and for great wealth. Hence, it was called "the great" (Dan. 4:20) and "the praise of the whole earth" (Jer. 51:41). However, the inhabitants were corrupt, licentious, and extremely immoral, worshiping idols and rejecting the true God.[77]

While God used Babylon to execute His judgment against Judah and His people, He did not leave Babylon unpunished for its many sins. The judgment of God against Babylon is spoken of many times in the Scriptures (see Isaiah 13; 14:22; 21:9; 47; Jeremiah 25; 50; 51). During the reign of Belshazzar, Nebuchadnezzar's grandson, the city was besieged and taken over by Cyrus (just as Daniel predicted the handwriting on the wall foretold, see Daniel 5). This was the beginning of the decline of Babylon. In the centuries that followed, the once mighty city was utterly abandoned and lost. Isaiah predicted that Babylon would be completely destroyed and never inhabited — "It will never be inhabited or lived in from generation to generation" (Is. 13:20). Such has been the case up until the present time.

The Bible contains many other fulfilled prophecies, from the invasion of Jerusalem to the fall of Rome. However, the most amazing example is seen in the life of Jesus Christ who fulfilled over 300 prophecies including: born of a virgin (Is. 7:14), time of birth (Dan. 9:25), from Bethlehem (Micah 5:2-5), hands and feet pierced (Ps. 22:16), lots cast for clothes (Ps. 22:18), mounted on a donkey (Zech. 9:9), suffering (Is. 53), betrayed by a friend (Ps. 41:9), betrayed for 30 pieces of silver (Zech. 11:12), His resurrection (Ps. 16:10), His ascension (Ps. 68:18). (For more see the chart on page 28, *Messianic Prophecies Fulfilled in Jesus Christ*.[78])

The chances of all of these being fulfilled in one person are astronomically large — one scientist gives odds of 10^{181}; another mathematician figured the odds were 10^{157} for fulfilling 48 prophecies.[79] Realizing there are only about 10^{74} atoms in the observable universe shows the magnitude of these numbers. To understand the size of 10^{181} consider: take a ball packed solidly with electrons (electrons are so small that a line of them one inch long would number 2½ quadrillion); expand the ball to the size of the universe (about 20 billion light years), multiply by 200 quadrillion. Remove one electron, color it red and stir it in. Blindfold a man and have him pick it out on the first try. Impossible? This is the same chance that Christ lived and died according to the Scripture by accident.[80]

Messianic Prophecies Fulfilled in Jesus Christ

Jesus claimed to be the object of fulfilled prophecy (Luke 24:27; Luke 24:44; John 5:39-40, 46-47; Luke 4:20-21; Luke 22:37). The Old Testament (O.T.) contains over 300 references to the Messiah that were fulfilled in Jesus and recorded in the New Testament (N.T.). Some of these include:

Prophecy	Prophecy in O.T.	Fulfilled in N.T.
Born of a virgin	Isaiah 7:14	Matt. 1:18, 24, 25
Born at Bethlehem	Micah 5:2	Matt. 2:1
Presented with gifts	Psalms 72:10	Matt. 2:1, 11
Ministry to begin in Galilee	Isaiah 9:1	Matt. 4:12, 13, 17
Ministry of miracles	Is. 35:5, 6a	Matt. 9:35
Teacher of parables	Ps. 78:2	Matt. 13:34
He was to enter Jerusalem on a donkey	Zech. 9:9	Luke 19:35-37
Betrayed by a friend	Ps. 42:9	Matt. 10:4
Sold for 30 pieces of silver	Zech. 11:12	Matt. 26:15
Money to be thrown in God's house	Zech. 11:13	Matt. 27:5
Forsaken by His disciples	Zech. 13:7	Mark 14:50
Accused by false witnesses	Ps. 35:11	Matt. 26:59-60
Dumb before accusers	Is. 53:7	Matt. 27:12
Wounded and bruised	Is. 53:5	Matt. 27:26
Smitten and spit upon	Is. 50:6	Matt. 26:67
Mocked	Ps. 22:7-8	Matt. 27:31
Hands and feet pierced	Ps. 22:16	Luke 23:33
Crucified with thieves	Is. 53:12	Matt. 27:38
Made intercession for His persecutors	Is. 53:12	Luke 23:34
Rejected by His own people	Is. 53:3	John 7:5, 48
Hated without a cause	Ps. 69:4	John 15:25
People shook their heads	Ps. 109:25	Matt. 27:39
Stared upon	Ps. 22:17	Luke 23:35
Garments parted and lots cast	Ps. 22:18	John 19:23-24
To suffer thirst	Ps. 69:21	John 19:28
Gall and vinegar offered him	Ps. 69:21	Matt. 27:34
His forsaken cry	Ps. 22:1	Matt. 27:46
Committed Himself to God	Ps. 31:5	Luke 23:46
Bones not broken	Ps. 34:20	John 19:33
Heart broken	Ps. 22:14	John 19:34
His side pierced	Zech. 12:10	John 19:34
Darkness over the land	Amos 8:9	Matt. 27:45
Buried in rich man's tomb	Is. 53:9	Matt. 27:57-60
His resurrection	Ps. 16:10	Acts 2:31
His ascension	Ps. 68:18	Acts 1:9

These did not happen by chance!

5. The Bible's Social Influence

The Bible has changed world history. No book has had such a positive impact on society. Wherever the Bible has gone and taken root and grown, it has changed cultures and nations. There are myriad examples, from the advance of Biblical Christianity in the first few centuries, to the transformation of Ireland and western Europe via Patrick and his Biblical training schools, to the continuing impact of the Protestant Reformation (the impetus for the birth of America) whose focal point was the Bible being made available in the common languages of the people.[81]

A microcosm of the Bible's transformational impact can be seen in the history of Pitcairn, an island in the South Pacific. After a group of mutineers took over the English ship *HMS Bounty* in 1789, some of them sought to hide on Pitcairn along with some natives they had befriended while in Tahiti. They were a motley crew — 9 white sailors, 6 Tahitian men, 10 women, and a girl of 15. One sailor discovered how to distill alcohol — drunkenness and fighting resulted. Soon only one white man was left with some of the native women and children. Alexander Smith found a Bible in a chest from the ship, and began to read it and teach what he learned. His life and everything on the island changed. When the U.S. ship Topaz landed on the island in 1808, they found a thriving, prosperous community with no whiskey, no jail, no crime, and no insane asylum. The application of the Bible changed this place from hell on earth to a good example of what God wants the world to be.

Biblical Christianity has impacted all spheres of life. Its transforming work has been like a mustard seed (Matt. 13:31-32) — it began small, but has become greater and greater throughout history. The impact the Bible has had upon the world is an indication of its divinity. No writing, religion, philosophy or person has ever even come close to affecting things as the Bible has. These have not just been "spiritual" or "religious" matters, but all areas of life. Some of those areas include:

1. The value of the individual

An engineer once asked his students, "What is the most important thing to come out of a mine?" Answers included gold, silver, copper, and diamonds. The teacher's response was "The most important thing to come out of a mine was the miner."[82] The Bible teaches that all men have great value because all men are created in the image of God. It teaches the equality of all men before the law. This Biblical view led to the end of slavery, the elevation of women, and representative government.

2. Compassion for the poor and needy

The Bible teaches that we are to love our neighbor as ourselves. Acting upon this precept motivated Christians to care for the poor, establish hospitals, and set up charitable organizations to meet the needs of fellow citizens. After serving those nearby, Christians went throughout the world doing similar acts of love. In fact, Christians are by far the greatest philanthropists in the world.

3. Education

The Bible teaches that everyone should have access to and know the truth, beginning with the Bible. This Biblical philosophy of education has motivated thousands of Christians to translate the Bible into myriads of languages, and where no written language existed, to first construct it. This idea is also the reason the church and Christians have established schools and universities wherever they go. In America, 106 of the fist 108 colleges were started by the church or Christian community.

4. Development of civil government

Civil liberty is a product of the Bible and Christian people. The great civil documents of liberty were almost universally written by Christians who looked to the Bible as the source of law.[83] In fact, the Bible being made available in the common language of a people preceded civil documents of liberty. Biblical ideas also gave rise to the framework of free governments, including such concepts as constitutionalism, separation of powers, limited government, separation of jurisdictions, and election of representatives.

King Alfred, who united and ruled England from 871-899, wrote a code of law based upon the Ten Commandments and Jesus' golden rule.

5. Emergence of individual rights and liberty

A Biblical view of man and government gave rise to the recognition and protection of God-given inalienable rights for mankind, including the rights to life, liberty, and property, as well as freedom of worship, speech, assembly, and the press. These freedoms are secured by the constitutions and civil documents originating in Christian societies.

6. Science and technology

The greatest scientists of all time were Christians or were a product of Christian societies. The Bible provided the worldview necessary for them to make their discoveries. (Many of these individuals were listed above.) The greatest inventions in history were also a product of Biblical men and thought, including the printing press, the steam engine, the reaper, the telegraph, and the electric motor, just to name a few.

7. Economics

Individual enterprise, private property, and free market principles are rooted in the Bible. Where these principles have been applied, economic prosperity has followed. The American Pilgrim founders demonstrated that Marxist socialist policies do not work. Their ability to reason from the Bible to economic affairs caused them to put aside communistic policies and embrace a free market system which elevated them out of poverty and set the foundation for great economic advancement. A father of the free market system and author of the classic *Wealth of Nations*, Adam Smith, was a Christian who derived his worldview from the Scriptures.

Adam Smith's economic principles were derived from the Bible.

8. Medicine

Advancements in medical care and discoveries occurred primarily in Christian societies. The discoverer of antiseptic surgery, Joseph Lister, was motivated by his Christian faith to find a way to limit hospital deaths due to infection.[84] The Biblical admonition to care for the sick prompted the establishment of hospitals and nursing, as well as groups like the Red Cross.

9. Moral advancement

Civilization has followed the spread of the Bible. Barbaric and primitive cultures have been civilized by Christianity, as witnessed in the early centuries of the Christian era in England, Ireland, and Scotland, and up through modern history as remote tribes have encountered Biblical Christianity. Oppressive societies have also been liberated by Biblical precepts.

10. Literature, arts and music

Where the Bible has gone, arts and the media have progressed. The father of modern musical notation, Monk Guido of Arezzo (995–1050), used a familiar hymn to teach notes via a mnemonic device (doh, re, mi, fa, sol, la). These notes were to music like the alphabet is to language. This instruction allowed the development of western music because now men could compose and pass on music, and explore music theory, harmony, and polyphony.[85] Many of the leading musicians and composers have been Christians, such as J.S. Bach and George F. Handel. Likewise, western art and painting developed out of a Christian worldview. The great authors of literature, history, theology, and politics were primarily Christians expressing the true nature of man and the universe in their writings.

The majority of people who made a significant contribution to advancements in all these fields have been Christians or a product of a Christian culture. The Bible shaped their lives and worldview, as well as the society at large.[86]

The Scripture informs us, "The unfolding of Thy words gives light; it gives understanding to the simple" (Psalm 119:130). The Bible gives laws for human relationships that have never been excelled or equaled. Where they have been taught and lived, they have transformed nations (Ireland, England, and the United States are examples). In languages where the Bible has been freely circulated, it has released astonishing power for good, overthrowing superstition and opening doors to progress in science, arts, humanities, inventions, and more. (South Korea is a modern example.[87])

The truth of the Bible has delivered hundreds of millions of people from fear, sickness, and sin. It has been and is the most powerful book for the renewal of man. Comparing the progress of nations in relation to their honoring the Bible and its Author shows: when they ignore, forget, or reject Him they have little growth and prosperity; when they love and apply the Bible to all of life, the nation advances, is exalted, and becomes prosperous.

To the degree that a people or nation applies the principles of the Bible is the degree to which that people or nation are free, prosperous, and advance in every sphere of life. Father of American Scholarship and Education, Noah Webster, stated:

> Almost all the civil liberty now enjoyed in the world owes its origin to the principles of the Christian religion....The religion which has introduced civil liberty, is the religion of Christ and his apostles, which enjoins humility, piety, and benevolence; which acknowledges in every person a brother, or a sister, and a citizen with equal rights. This is genuine Christianity, and to this we owe our free constitutions of government.[88]

To summarize, "Happy is the nation whose God is the Lord" (Psalm 33:12).

6. The Bible's Supreme Appeal

The message of the Bible is universal. It applies to all men in all places throughout all history. Both the child and the scholar will delight in it. Its simple life-related principles work in any culture. Only the Bible, and its living message, can make bad men good inside, transforming the rebel to a saint — with innumerable examples of this occurring throughout history. The appeal is so great that many gladly face persecution and even martyrdom to cling to its message.

It appeals to all men — the orphan in the Ukraine, the woman in Afghanistan, the leader in western government, the tribesman in a remote region of Africa, the wealthy investor in America, the uneducated in the Amazon jungle as well as the most educated professor in the academic jungle, college students and military men, those on their death bed as well as the young child. All of these have embraced the life transforming message of the Bible and benefitted from the fruit of obedience to its principles.

Its supreme appeal has been demonstrated by the rapid growth of the Christian faith in the past few centuries, and especially in the last half century as its message has spread all over the world. Consider these statistics: the ratio of Christian to total world population in 1430 was 1 to 99; in 1790, it was 1 to 49; in 1940, 1 to 32; in 1994, 1 to 7; and today, 1 in 3 people in the world are nominally Christian, and at least one in ten are Bible-believing Christians. Following are the current estimated percentages of the population of various nations who are "renewalists" (that is, they have a living Christian faith and are not just nominal Christians): Guatemala, 60%; Kenya, 56%; Brazil, 49%; Philippines, 44%; South Africa, 34%; Chile, 30%; Nigeria, 26%; United States, 23%; Colombia, 20%; South Korea, over 20%. Most of this growth (other than in the U.S.) has come in the last 3-4 decades.[89] As one church historian wrote, "the growth of the church since 1950 is so remarkable as to be without precedent in the history of the world."[90] That growth is taking place among many different people groups.

The diverse appeal of the Biblical message is especially revealed today in the impact it is having among those with a Muslim background. Longtime Muslim missionary and author Tom Doyle believes "more Muslims have become followers of Jesus in the last ten years than in the last fourteen centuries of Islam."[91] In addition to anecdotal stories, there is objective evidence of a genuine move of God occurring today within Muslim lands. This revival has been documented by David Garrison in *A Wind in the House of Islam*. He records that across 29 nations where most of the world's 1.6 billion Muslims live, there have been 82 movements to Christianity from Islam, defined by at least 100 new churches or 1000 baptisms – and 84% of them have happened since 2000.[92] While it is difficult to get accurate figures, perhaps 5-10 million Muslims have become Christians in the last five years in the Middle East. The Iranian Christian population is 1-3 million. Most have never been to church but are being reached by TV, radio, and internet.[93]

7. The Bible's Supernatural Salvation

The greatest proof of the divine nature of the Bible is the difference its message makes in lives. Its central message is that Jesus Christ transforms men from spiritual death to life. For 2000 years Jesus has delivered individuals from the kingdom of darkness into the kingdom of light – men and women of all ages, from all types of cultural backgrounds, with all levels of education, wealth, and social status. He regenerates them and then transforms them.

He satisfies the spiritual hunger in man: "Whoever drinks of the water that I shall give him shall never thirst" (John 4:14). "Jesus said to them, 'I am the bread of life; he who comes to Me shall not hunger, and he who believes in Me shall never thirst'" (John 6:35). "I came that they might have life, and might have it abundantly" (John 10:10). "Come to Me, all who are weary and heavy-laden, and I will give you rest" (Matt. 11:28).

The testimonies of myriads of those converted have been recorded. Many of these people are well known, such as the Apostle Paul, Augustine, Patrick of Ireland, Martin Luther, Pocahontas, John Newton, John Wesley, Noah Webster, Cyrus McCormick, Charles Finney, James Garfield, Sgt. York, and Chuck Colson. Others are lesser known, like Jacob Deshazer, Bob Hite, Louis Zamperini, and Mitsuo Fuchida.[94] The stories of the vast majority of those converted to Christ are only written in the Book of Life. Following are a few testimonies revealing the transforming power of the Bible.

John Wesley

John was the thirteenth child of Samuel and Susannah Wesley. His father was a minister that suffered much persecution for his faith. As a child John was miraculously saved from a fire. He later wrote that he was "a brand plucked from the burning." Through his parental training and personal education, God imparted to John the desire to change the world. He set out to do so, even before he was converted, by going as a missionary in 1735 to the new colony of Georgia in America. After witnessing the Moravians' faith in a storm at sea, he sought counsel from the Moravian pastor on his own conduct.

The Bible: Divine or Human? 35

[The pastor] said, "Do you know Jesus Christ?" I paused and said, "I know He is the Savior of the world." "True," the pastor replied, "but do you know He has saved you?" I answered, "I hope He has died to save me." He added, "Do you know yourself?" I said, "I do." In recollecting the event, I thought, "But I fear they were vain words."[95]

After a few years in Georgia with no success, Wesley returned home. On the homeward journey he recorded in his diary:

John Wesley's heart was "strangely warmed" by the living God.

I went to America to convert the Indians; but oh, who shall convert me?...I have a fair summer religion; I can talk well...and believe myself while no danger is near. But let death stare me in the face and my spirit is troubled, nor can I say to die is gain.[96]

On February 1, 1738, the day he landed in England, he wrote:

It is now two years and four months since I left my native country in order to teach the Georgian Indians the nature of Christianity; but what have I learned of myself in the meantime? Why, what I least suspected; that I who went to America to convert others was never myself converted to God! I am not mad, though I thus speak, but I speak the words of truth and soberness.[97]

For three months Wesley went to meetings, studied Scripture, and prayed in pursuit of God. On Wednesday May 24, 1738, Wesley was at a prayer meeting on Aldersgate Street, listening to Luther's Preface to Romans. He writes:

About a quarter to nine, while he was describing the change which God works in the heart through faith in Christ, I felt my heart strangely warmed. I felt I did trust Christ, Christ alone for salvation; and an assurance was given me that He had taken away my sins, even mine, and saved me from the law of sin and death.[98]

From this point on, his ministry changed. He began to preach the doctrine of instantaneous conversion and justification through faith in Christ. Many were now converted to Christ in his meetings. The Holy Spirit had made the central message of the Bible real to him.

Charles Finney

Charles Finney (1792-1875) was the central figure in the later part of the Second Great Awakening. One biographer wrote of him:

> When he opened his mouth he was aiming a gun. When he spoke bombardment began. The effects of his speaking were almost unparalleled in modern history. Over half a million people were converted through his ministry…in an age when there were no amplifiers or mass communications, he spearheaded a revival which literally altered the course of history.[99]

As a young man, Finney attended church, but he scorned prayer meetings because he "never saw any of their prayers answered." While studying to become a lawyer he read Blackstone's *Law Commentaries*, and was struck by the constant references to the Bible as the basis of all civil and moral law. Because of this he began to seriously study the Bible. He later wrote of his thoughts as he began to confront the ideas in this book:

> I often said to myself "If these things are really taught in the Bible, I must be an infidel." But the more I read my Bible the more clearly I saw that these things were not found there upon any fair principles of interpretation such as would be admitted in a court of justice….But the Spirit of God conducted me through the darkness and delivered me from the labyrinth and fog of a false philosophy, and set my feet upon the rock of truth — as I trust.[100]

Finney had a dramatic conversion, which he relates in detail in his autobiography. After encountering the living Christ and being filled powerfully with the Holy Spirit—which occurred over several days—and feeling a call to the ministry, God immediately began to use him to impact others.

Charles Finney

His conversion took place in October of 1821. In the days following he experienced, as he wrote, "a mighty baptism of the Holy Ghost" where "the Holy Spirit descended on me in a manner that seemed to go through me, body and soul. I could feel the impression, like a wave of electricity, going through and through me. Indeed, I could not express it any other way. It seemed like the very breath of God. I can recall distinctly that it seemed to fan me like immense wings."[101]

The next day after this, each encounter he had with the lost led to powerful conviction and conversion. "The first man he spoke to, (his boss, a Judge) was struck with such conviction of sin that he could not look at him. He left the office under deep conviction, and a few days later was converted in the same woods where Finney himself was saved. The second visitor, a client and a church deacon with a 10:00 a.m. case for the newly converted barrister to try for him, did not escape either. The young lawyer met him with the words, 'I have a retainer from the Lord Jesus Christ to plead His cause and I cannot plead yours.' The next, a Universalist in a Christian shoemaker's shop had his arguments demolished, and headed over the fence to the woods and salvation. From that day on, Finney realized it was goodbye to his legal profession. He launched out on a life of fire and power such as there have been few parallels in Christian history."[102]

Noah Webster

Called the Father of American Scholarship and Education, Noah Webster (1758-1843) affected the course of education in early America more than any other person. He authored numerous books including the "Blue-Back Speller" (which sold over 100 million copies), the first exhaustive English dictionary, a grammar, a reader, and a United States history. In addition, he translated his own version of the Bible, helped to found a college, started the first magazine in America, and was the first person to publicly promote a constitutional convention.

Webster's dictionary contains thousands of scriptural references and gives Biblical definitions.

For the first fifty years of Webster's life, he was a God-fearing, moral man who studied the Scriptures, attended church, and looked at life primarily from a Biblical perspective. Yet, it was not until 1808, shortly after his beginning work on the dictionary, that Webster repented and accepted salvation by faith.

That year, as revival swept through New Haven, his wife and two eldest daughters were three of the first to have their lives transformed. At first, Webster tried to rationalize what happened to his family as mere over-enthusiasm, but as the weeks went by his mind was more and more filled with thoughts of God, making his studies very difficult.

Webster described what happened one day while at his studies in a letter to his brother-in-law, Judge Thomas Dawes:

> My mind was suddenly arrested, without any previous circumstance of the time to draw it to this subject and, as it were, fastened to the awakening and upon my own conduct. I closed my books, yielded to the influence which could not be resisted or mistaken, and was led by a spontaneous impulse to repentance, prayer, and entire submission and surrender of myself to my Maker and Redeemer. My submission appeared to be cheerful, and was soon followed by that peace of mind which the world can neither give nor take away.[103]

His already developed diligence is revealed by his action immediately following this, for "he instantly made known to his family the feelings which he entertained. He called them together the next morning and told them, with deep emotion, that, while he had aimed at the faithful discharge of all his duties as their parent and head, he had neglected one of the most important, that of family prayer. After reading the Scriptures, he led them, with deep solemnity, to the throne of grace, and from that time continued the practice, with the liveliest interest, to the period of his death."[104]

The first versions of *An American Dictionary of the English Language* published after the author's death contained a short biography of Noah Webster by his son-in-law Chauncy A. Goodrich. Webster's conversion and faith were clearly presented in this work and would have been read by many, many Americans.[105]

John Colby, Daniel Webster's Brother-in-Law

The Biblical message of Christ's redemption can make wicked men good. Daniel Webster (1782-1852) — who served as a Congressman, Senator, and Secretary of State for three Presidents — attested to the supernatural transformation that can only come from the living God of the Bible.

Daniel Webster's older sister had married a man, John Colby, who was thought to be a fine citizen but turned out to be far from it. Over time he became more difficult, profane, and impious. He was called "the wickedest man in the neighborhood."[106] Webster was young when he met him but lost touch when John and his sister moved away, and when his sister died after five or six years there was no interaction at all. Decades later Webster heard that John had become a Christian and so he decided one day to visit him to see if that were so.

He told a friend who was going with him the reason for his visit to see John Colby: "I have been told by persons who know, that, within a few years, he has become a convert to the Christian religion, and has met with that mysterious change which we call a change of heart; in other words, he has become a constant, praying Christian. This has given me a very strong desire to have a personal interview with him, and to hear with my own ears his account of this change. For, humanly speaking, I should have said that his was about as hopeless a case for conversion as I could well conceive."[107]

Daniel and his companion traveled to the village where he lived, found his home, and began introductions. John Colby did not recognize Daniel as he was a youth the last time he had seen him. Once he learned who he was John expressed great surprise, never thinking he would see him again, especially considering Daniel was one of the most well known men in the nation. John said he regularly heard about him in the papers and then stated:

> They say that you are a great man, that you are a famous man; and you can't tell how delighted I am when I hear such things. But, Daniel, the time is short, – you won't stay here long, – I want to ask you one important question. You may be a great man; are you a good man? Are you a Christian man? Do you love the Lord Jesus Christ? That is the only question that is worth asking or answering. Are you a Christian? You know, Daniel, what I have been: I have been one of the wickedest of men. Your poor sister, who is now in heaven, knows that. But the spirit of Christ and of Almighty God has come down and plucked me as a brand from the everlasting burning. I am here now, a monument to his grace. Oh, Daniel I would not give what is contained within the covers of this book [speaking of a Scott's Family Bible on the table] for all the honors that have been conferred upon men from the creation of the world until now. For what good would it do? It is nothing, and less than nothing, if you are not a Christian, if you are not repentant. If you do not love the Lord Jesus Christ, in sincerity and truth, all your worldly honors will sink to utter nothingness. Are you a Christian? Do you love Christ?

Daniel responded by professing he was a Christian and did trust in the grace of God for salvation, but also expressed the need for a deeper faith, one with as much earnestness as John seemed to have. Webster then expressed "how much delight it gave me to hear of your conversion. The hearing of that is what has led me here today. I came here to see with my own eyes, and hear with my own ears the story from a man that I know and remember well. What a wicked man you used to be!" John Colby exclaimed:

> O Daniel! You don't remember how wicked I was; how ungrateful I was; how unthankful I was! I never thought of God; I never cared for God; I was worse than the heathen. Living in a Christian land, with the light shining all around me, and the blessings of Sabbath teachings everywhere about me, I was worse than a heathen until I was arrested by the grace of Christ, and made to see my sinfulness, and to hear the voice of my Saviour.[108]

Daniel Webster said that the supernatural transformation of his brother-in-law testified of the living God of the Bible.

John asked for prayer, they knelt down and Webster "offered a most touching and eloquent prayer," after which John prayed for Daniel and everybody present. When they left later that day Webster remarked to his companion:

> I should like to know what the enemies of religion would say to John Colby's conversion. There was a man as unlikely, humanly speaking, to become a Christian as any man I ever saw. He was reckless, heedless, impious; never attended church, never experienced the good influence of associating with religious people. And here he has been living on in that reckless way until he has got to be an old man; until a period of life when you naturally would not expect his habits to change: and yet he has been brought into the condition in which we have seen him today,—a penitent, trusting, humble believer. Whatever people may say, nothing…can convince me that any thing short of the grace of Almighty God could make such a change as I, with my own eyes, have witnessed in the life of John Colby.[109]

That evening he remarked to another friend that "miracles happen in these later days as well as in the days of old." When asked what was he referencing Webster said, "Why, John Colby has become a Christian. If that is not a miracle, what is?"[110]

Supernatural transformations similar to those experienced by Colby, Hite, DeShazer, Webster, Finney, and Wesley have occurred in hundreds of millions of people throughout the Christian era. They add powerful support to the fact that the Bible is the divine, inerrant, inspired Word of God. No other religion can point to such internal change with even one adherent.

The Value of the Bible

Only Christianity – the religion of the Bible – supernaturally changes the heart and lives of people. The same supernatural power that saved us is also needed for us to grow in grace and be changed into the image of the living God. Once we are saved, the Bible continues to provide the knowledge and principles we need to walk out our salvation. For all aspects of salvation, we need the Spirit of God to illuminate our hearts and minds to understand. We cannot discover and see the truth on our own.

Many have read and studied the Bible and have not been converted and enlightened. This has caused some to reject the divine nature of the book. (Even so, many unbelievers have recognized and appreciated the content of the Bible, including Thomas Jefferson and Benjamin Franklin.) God has promised to answer the earnest seeker. If we are willing to do His will, He will reveal God's teachings to us (John 7:17). Bible truth must be revealed by the Holy Spirit: "Then He (Jesus) opened their minds to understand the Scriptures" (Luke 24:45). John the Baptist said, "A man can receive nothing, unless it has been given him from heaven" (John 3:27). Jesus said: "I praise Thee, O Father, Lord of heaven and earth, that Thou didst hide these things from the wise and intelligent and didst reveal them to babes" (Luke 10:21).

A Mr. Watso once said: "A man may read the figures on the dial, but he cannot tell how the day goes unless the sun is shining on it; so we may read the Bible over, but we cannot learn to purpose till the Spirit of God shine upon it and into our hearts." It is the Spirit-applied word that cleanses us: "that He [Jesus] might sanctify her [the church], having cleansed her by the washing of water with the word" (Eph. 5:26).

Life goes much better when we have a great amount of the Spirit-applied Word in our lives. Many years ago I went on a canoe trip on a small river when the water level was low. Consequently, there were many bumps from rocks just below the water level, and we hit many exposed rocks. Numerous times we had to get out and push and pick up the canoe. We almost tipped over multiple times. To complete the trip we had to exert much energy. Traversing the same river with high water is completely different. When the water is high, we run swiftly in the fast places and flow gently in the slow places, but can manage easily if we handle the paddles right (we are to handle accurately the word of truth, 2 Tim. 2:15). We will not turn over unless we get out of balance (which is true with the Christian life as well). The water level of the river corresponds to the amount of Spirit-applied Word in our lives.

The Bible **is** the Word of Almighty God. It is our source of what we know to be truth and the foundation of our epistemology (the study of truth). It is our life-manual, the manufacturer's handbook. The Bible is the most important book in the world. It holds the key to life and every problem. As Psalm 19:7-11 declares:

> The law of the Lord is perfect, converting the soul: the testimony of the Lord is sure, making wise the simple. The statutes of the Lord are right, rejoicing the heart: the commandment of the Lord is pure, enlightening the eyes. The fear of the Lord is clean, enduring for ever: the judgments of the Lord are true and righteous altogether. More to be desired are they than gold, yea, than much fine gold; sweeter also than honey and the honeycomb. Moreover by them is Thy servant warned: and in keeping of them there is great reward.

The 119th Psalm, which is by far the longest, explains the eminence, magnificence, power, guidance, and life of God's Word. A few of those verses include:

> How can a young man keep his way pure? By keeping it according to Thy word. With all my heart I have sought Thee; do not let me wander from Thy commandments. Thy word have I treasured (hid) in mine heart, that I might not sin against Thee. Blessed art Thou, O LORD; teach me Thy statutes. With my lips have I declared all the judgments of Thy mouth. I have rejoiced in the way of Thy testimonies, as much as in all riches. I will meditate in Thy precepts, and have respect unto Thy ways. I will delight myself in Thy statutes; I will not forget Thy word (v. 9-16).
>
> Forever, O LORD, Thy word is settled in heaven (v. 89).
>
> O how I love Thy law! It is my meditation all the day. Thy commandments make me wiser than my enemies, for they are ever with me. I have more understanding than all my teachers, for Thy testimonies are my meditation. I understand more than the aged, because I keep Thy precepts. I have refrained my feet from every evil way, that I might keep Thy word. I have not departed from Thy judgments, for Thou Thyself hast taught me. How sweet are Thy words to my taste! Yes sweeter than honey to my mouth! Through Thy precepts I get understanding; therefore I hate every false way. Thy word is a lamp unto my feet, and a light unto my path (v. 97-105).
>
> The entrance of Thy words gives light; it gives understanding to the simple (v. 130).

> The sum of Thy word is truth, and every one of Thy righteous ordinances is everlasting (v. 160).
>
> Those who love Thy law have great peace, and nothing causes them to stumble[111] (v. 165).

Since God's Word is of such value, we need to **read the Word, research the Word, meditate upon the Word**, and **memorize the Word**. It is our spiritual food:

> But He [Jesus] answered and said, "It is written, man shall not live by bread alone, but by every word that proceeds out of the mouth of God (Matt. 4:4).

> I have treasured the words of His mouth more than my necessary food (Job 23:12).
>
> Thy words were found, and I ate them, and Thy words became for me a joy and the delight of my heart (Jeremiah 15:16).

We need to find His words, eat them, and store them in our heart. We need to apply them personally and in our families, schools, businesses, communities, and nation. Jesus reveals why they should become the foundation of our lives and our nations in Matthew 7:24-27:

> Every one therefore that hears these words of Mine, and does them, may be compared to a wise man, who built his house upon the rock. And the rain descended, and the floods came, and the winds blew, and beat upon that house; and yet it did not fall, for it was founded upon the rock. And every one that hears these words of Mine, and does not do them, will be like a foolish man, who built his house upon the sand. And the rain descended, and the floods came, and the winds blew, and burst against that house; and it fell, and great was its fall.

We should build our houses (lives, thinking, worldview) upon the rock (God's truth/word) and not upon the sand (false ideologies) because a house built upon the rock will stand during the storms of life, but a house built upon the sand will crumble.

The Bible is the source of God's truth to mankind. It is the source for experiencing great blessings for all of life. The Spirit-applied Word of God – the living Bible – reveals all that is important about our existence, here in the earth and for the eternal hereafter. It is the source of truth, correct knowledge of God and man, and tells us why we are here and what we are to be doing in the earth. Obedience to His Word is the difference between being a nominal Christian and a true believer. Obedience to the Bible is how we show our love for Him. To obey is also smart because adherence to the Bible's precepts brings great life, liberty, and blessings. This is because the Bible is inspired, inerrant, and divine.

End Notes

[1] We are working to give a copy of this book to all 7383 state legislators in all 50 states. To date, copies have been (or will be) distributed to one or both houses in ten states. To learn more about this project and how you can help reach leaders see: http://providencefoundation.com/?page_id=4041

[2] See for example: Wayne Grudem's *Systematic Theology* and Millard J. Erickson's *Christian Theology* for two recent works.

[3] Craig Nelson, *The First Heroes, the Extraordinary Story of the Doolittle Raid – America's First World War II Victory*, Penguin Book, 2003, p. 303.

[4] Ibid.

[5] Ibid.

[6] Ibid., p. 304.

[7] Ibid.

[8] Ibid., p. 305.

[9] See Nelson, pp. 342, 347 ff.

[10] The word *Bible* comes from the Greek *Biblia*, (a form of *biblos* meaning book) which comes from *byblos* (papyrus); papyrus was used to make paper for books. *Biblia* is used in the LXX (Septuagint, the Greek translation of the Old Testament) for Scriptures (Dan. 9:2); by the 5th century Greek church fathers applied *biblia* to the whole Christian Scripture; in Latin it became singular to "The Book." In the New Testament the Old Testament is usually referred to as "the Scriptures."

[11] The inerrancy of the Bible applies to the original manuscripts of the Old and New Testaments, i.e. the autographs. All copies and translations of the Bible are inerrant to the degree they represent the autographs. While the original autographs are not known to exist, thousands of copies that originated from the autographs exist, and there agreement with one another is such that we know that over 99% of the words of the Bible are what the original manuscript said. (see Wayne Grudem, *Systemic Theology*, Grand Rapids: Inter-Varsity Press and Zondervan Publishing House, 1994, p. 96.)

[12] For a brief Biblical view of each of these areas see Stephen McDowell, *Equal Justice Under God's Law, Building Nations with the Blueprint of God's Word*, Charlottesville: Providence Foundation, 2010.

[13] Clement of Rome First letter to the Corinthians XLV, quoted at https://answersingenesis.org/is-the-bible-true/why-should-we-believe-in-the-inerrancy-of-scripture/

[14] Irenaeus, Against Heresies, XVII.2, at https://answersingenesis.org/is-the-bible-true/why-should-we-believe-in-the-inerrancy-of-scripture/

[15] A Treatise on the Soul, 21, in ANF, 3:202 at https://fromthestudy.com/2014/10/13/inerrancy-and-church-history-the-early-fathers/

[16] Letters, 82, in NPNF, 1:350 in ibid.

[17] *The Book of Confessions*, Louisville: The Office of the General Assembly of the Presbyterian Church, 2002, p. 3.

[18] https://en.wikipedia.org/wiki/Biblical_inerrancy

[19] "The Scots Confession," 1560, in *The Book of Confessions*, p. 20.

[20] "The Second Helvetic Confessions," 1561, in *The Book of Confessions*, p., 53.

[21] "The Confession of Faith," in *The Constitution of the Presbyterian Church in the United States*, Richmond: Presbyterian Committee of Publication, 1932, p. xxv.

[22] "The Westminster Larger Catechism," in *The Constitution of the Presbyterian Church in the United States*, p. 168, answer to question 3. Scriptures given are Gal. 1: 8-9; Isa. 8:20; Luke 16:29, 31; 2 Tim. 3:15-17.

[23] Calvin, reflecting the view of the Reformers, believed that God speaks to man via the Bible and therefore, "we owe to the Scriptures the same reverence which we owe to God." (Quoted in Charles Colson, *Loving God*, Grand Rapids: Zondervan, 1987, p. 71.)

[24] "The Chicago Statement on Biblical Inerrancy, A Short Statement," *Rebuilding Civilization on the Bible*, Ventura, Cal.: Nordskog Publishing, 2014, p. 19.

[25] John Locke, Letter to the Right Reverend Edward, Lord Bishop of Worcester, 7 January 1696-97; *The Works of John Locke in Nine Volumes* (Rivington, 1824; 12th ed.) vol. 3, in John Eidsmoe, *Historical and Theological Foundations of Law, Vol. III*, Powder Springs Press: American Vision Press, 2011, p. 1162.

[26] Sir William Blackstone, *Commentaries on the Laws of England*, Philadelphia: Robert Bell, Union Library, 1771, vol. 1, 38-42.

[27] For more on this see Stephen McDowell, *The Bible: America's Source of Law and Liberty*, Charlottesville: Providence Foundation, 2016.

[28] "An Answer to the Question, Why do you attend a Unitarian Church?" (Published at the Christian Register Office, John B. Russell, printer), circa 1840, in David Barton, *Original Intent*, Aledo, Tex.: WallBuilder Press, 2002, p. 314.

[29] William Bradford, *Of Plymouth Plantation*, written 1621-1650, reprinted by Vision Forum, 1998, p. 163.

[30] *The Laws of the Pilgrims, A Facsimile Edition of The Book of the General Laws of the Inhabitants of the Jurisdiction of New – Plimouth, 1672 & 1685,* Wilmington, Del.: Michael Glazier, Inc., 1977.

[31] *Sources of Our Liberties*, edited by Richard L. Perry, Chicago: American Bar Foundation, 1959, p. 120.

[32] *Colonial Origins of the American Constitution*, edited by Donald S. Lutz, Indianapolis: Liberty Fund, 1998, p. 222.

[33] *Sources of Our Liberties*, p. 148.

[34] *The Constitutions of the Several Independent States of America*, Boston: Norman and Bowen, 1785, pp. 99-100, Delaware, 1776, Article 22. See also, Constitution of Delaware 1776 Article 22, http://avalon.law.yale.edu/18th_century/de02.asp

[35] http://avalon.law.yale.edu/18th_century/pa08.asp

[36] From Gallup reports, in Charles Colson, *Loving God*, p. 72.

[37] Lifeway Research survey of 1000 Americans in September 2014, in *World Magazine*, November 14, 2015, p. 61. The same survey showed 28% of Americans believed "following the Quran's teachings would be good for American society."

[38] David Kinnaman and Gabe Lyons, *Good Faith, Being a Christian When Society Thinks You're Irrelevant and Extreme*, Grand Rapids: Baker Books, 2016, p. 226.

[39] John Jay, *John Jay: The Winning of the Peace, Unpublished Papers 1780-1784*, Richard B. Morris, editor, New York: Harper & Row Publishers, 1980, Vol. 2, p. 709.

[40] *Letters of John Quincy Adams to His Son on the Bible and Its Teachings,* Auburn: James M. Alden, 1850, pp. 9-21.

[41] Edward Beardsley, *Life and Times of William Samuel Johnson,* Boston: Houghton, Mifflin and Company, 1886, pp. 141-142.

[42] Quoted in David Barton, *Original Intent,* Aledo, Tex.: WallBuilder Press, 2002, p. 7.

[43] Lewis Henry Boutell, *The Life of Roger Sherman,* Chicago: A.C. McClurg and Company, 1896, p. 272.

[44] Noah Webster, *Value of the Bible and Excellence of the Christian Religion,* 1834, republished by the Foundation for American Christian Education, San Francisco, 1988, p. 79.

[45] William Wirt, *Sketches of the Life and Character of Patrick Henry,* Philadelphia: James Webster, publisher, 1818, p. 402.

[46] See Stephen McDowell, *In God We Trust Tour Guide,* Charlottesville: Providence Foundation, 1998, p. 169, and R. Watson, *An Apology for the Bible, in a Series of Letters Addressed to Thomas Paine, Author of the Age of Reason,* New York: J. Emory and S. Waugh, 1832.

[47] For more see McDowell, *The Bible: America's Source of Law and Liberty,* Chapter 3.

[48] Andrew W. Young, *First Lessons in Civil Government,* Auburn, N.Y.: H. And J.C. Ivison, 1846, p. 16.

[49] *American Eloquence: A Collection of Speeches and Addresses, by the Most Eminent Orators of America,* Frank Moore, editor, New York: D. Appleton and Co., 1858, Vol. 2, p. 263.

[50] Noah Webster, *An American Dictionary of the English Language,* 1828, Facsimile edition republished by the Foundation for American Christian Education, San Francisco, 1980, definition of the Bible.

[51] Winkie Pratney, *Youth Aflame,* Lindale, Tex.: Communication Foundation Publishers, 1970, p. 209.

[52] Ibid.

[53] Jesus is the Word made flesh (John 1). God came into the world as a man, Jesus Christ. The life and influence of Jesus reflects what you might expect would happen if God became man. If God became man, then we would expect him to: 1) Have an unusual entrance into life — virgin birth. 2) Be without sin. 3) Manifest the supernatural in the form of miracles. 4) Have an acute sense of difference from other men. 5) Speak the greatest words ever spoken. 6) Have a lasting and universal influence. 7) Satisfy the spiritual hunger in man. 8) Exercise power over death. [James Kennedy, *What If Jesus Had Never Been Born?* Nashville: Thomas Nelson Publishers, 1994, p.111 ff]

[54] See Josh McDowell, *Evidence that Demands a Verdict,* for a discussion on this.

[55] Wayne Grudem, *Systematic Theology,* p. 74.

[56] Grudem, p. 57.

[57] Westminster Confession of Faith, p. 13.

[58] Some people argue that the idea that Scripture is self-attesting is circular reasoning. However, "all arguments for an absolute authority must ultimately appeal to that authority for proof" (Grudem, p. 78). Christians appeal to the Bible as the ultimate authority. Fallen man usually appeals to himself since he considers man to be ultimate. The belief that man is the ultimate one has no supporting evidence, unlike the belief in the divinity of the Bible which has abundant supporting evidence. (For more on self-attestation see Grudem, p. 78-80.)

[59] The seven general points presented in this section are from Winkie Pratney, *Youth Aflame,* pp. 212-215. These points are not unique to Pratney as they have been given by many people during the past centuries as support for the divine nature of the Bible.

[60] *Canonization* is the term used to describe the process of the compilation of the books that belong to the Bible. To learn more about the canon of Scripture see, Wayne Grudem, *Systematic Theology*, pp. 54-71.

[61] *Foxe's Book of Martyrs*, Edited by Marie Gentert King, Old Tappan, New Jersey: Fleming H. Revell Co., 1978. Jock Purves, *Fair Sunshine, Character Studies of the Scottish Covenanters*, Carlisle, Penn.: The Banner of Truth Trust, 1990. James and Marti Hefley, *By Their Blood, Christian Martyrs of the 20th Century*, Milford, Mich.: Mott Media, 1979.

[62] Darrel L. Bock, *Can I Trust the Bible?* Norcross, Ga.: RZIM. In years past various critics would discount the Old Testament texts as originating from the pre-Christian era (especially those texts prophesying of Christ the Messiah) since the oldest Hebrew texts dated only to the 900s AD. But in 1946 (and in the years following to 1956) the Dead Sea Scrolls were found in eleven caves about 2 kilometers inland from the northwest shore of the Dead Sea. These scrolls date from the third century BC and contain hundreds of portions of the Old Testament (as well as some other writings). Scrolls found include all of Isaiah and parts of all the other Old Testament books except Esther.

[63] https://en.wikipedia.org/wiki/List_of_best-selling_books. http://www.christianuniversitiesonline.org/the-bible/

[64] Pratney, p. 211.

[65] The Bible was first divided into chapters and verses in 1227 AD. The Geneva Bible (1560) was the first English Bible so divided.

[66] Pratney, p. 212.

[67] Ibid.

[68] Ibid.

[69] Charles Lee Lewis, *Matthew Fontaine Maury, The Pathfinder of the Seas*, New York: AMS Press, 1969 (reprinted from edition of 1927), p. 218.

[70] Lewis, pp. 98-99.

[71] Maury wrote: "As a student of physical geography I regard the earth, sea, air and water as parts of a machine, pieces of mechanism not made by hands, but to which, nevertheless, certain offices have been assigned in the terrestrial economy. It is good and profitable to seek to find out these offices, and point them out to our fellows; and when, after patient research, I am led to the discovery of any one of them, I feel with the astronomer of old as though I had 'thought one of God's thoughts!' — and tremble." (Hidlegarde Hawthorne, *Matthew Fontaine Maury, Trail Maker of the Seas*, New York: Longmans, Green and Co., 1943, pp. 154-155.)

[72] Lewis, pp. 251-252.

[73] James Rose, *A Guide to American Christian Education*, Camarillo, CA: American Christian History Institute, 1987, 455.

[74] Pratney, p. 213.

[75] See for example: http://www.biblearchaeology.org/bookstore/?gclid=CMmcq6vs48sCFRJZhgod9lsPLQ; http://www.equip.org/article/biblical-archaeology-factual-evidence-to-support-the-historicity-of-the-bible/; http://www.christianitytoday.com/ct/2014/december-web-only/biblical-archaeologys-top-ten-discoveries-of-2014.html

[76] Pratney, p. 213.

[77] *International Bible Dictionary*, Plainfield, New Jersey: Logos International, 1977, 49.

[78] See Josh McDowell, *Evidence for Christianity*, Nashville: Thomas Nelson, 2006, Chapter 6, "Old Testament Prophecies Fulfilled in Jesus Christ," pp. 193 ff.

[79] *Science Speaks*, Chicago: Moody Press, 1958, 100-107.

[80] Pratney, p. 214.
[81] To learn about these events and others see Mark Beliles and Stephen McDowell, *America's Providential History*, Charlottesville: Providence Foundation, 2010. Stephen McDowell, *Monumental: Restoring America as the Land of Liberty*, Libertyman Publishers, 2014. Stephen McDowell, *Biblical Revival and the Transformation of Nations*, Charlottesville: Providence Foundation, 2013.
[82] D. James Kennedy and Jerry Newcombe, *What If Jesus Had Never Been Born?* p. 9.
[83] See McDowell, *The Bible: America's Source of Law and Liberty*.
[84] See Stephen McDowell, *Transforming Medicine and Business with Biblical Principles*, Charlottesville: Providence Foundation, 2010.
[85] Kennedy, p. 182-183.
[86] For a list of many of the leaders see Stephen McDowell, *Building Godly Nations*, Chapter 1, Charlottesville: Providence Foundation, 2003.
[87] See McDowell, *The Bible: America's Source of Law and Liberty*, pp. 72-75.
[88] Noah Webster, *History of the United States*, New Haven: Durrie & Peck, 1833, pp. 273-4.
[89] See various studies: http://www.pewforum.org/Christian/Global-Christianity-movements-and-denominations.aspx; and http://www.gordonconwell.edu/resources/Center-for-the-Study-of-Global-Christianity.cfm
[90] Grudem, p. 1124.
[91] Tom Doyle and Greg Webster, *Dreams and Visions, Is Jesus Awakening the Muslim World?*, Nashville: Thomas Nelson, p. xiv-xv.
[92] From article by Mindy Belz in *World Magazine*, May 31, 2014, summarizing findings in *A Wind in the House of Islam* (2014) by David Garrison.
[93] Personal report from representative of Alkarma Satellite TV, March 5, 2015.
[94] For some of these stories see: Stephen McDowell, *Biblical Revival and the Transformation of Nations*; http://providencefoundation.com/wp-content/uploads/2011/08/May-07-Persp-Alvin-York.pdf; http://providencefoundation.com/?page_id=2497 (Fuchida's story).
[95] Wesley Journals, quoted in Winkie Pratney, *Revival, Principles to Change the World*, Springdale, Penn.: Whitaker House, 1983, p. 69.
[96] Wesley Journals, quoted in Pratney, p. 69.
[97] Wesley Journals, quoted in Pratney, p. 69.
[98] Wesley Journals, quoted in Pratney, p. 70.
[99] Edward Miller, *Charles Finney*, quoted in Pratney, p. 116.
[100] Charles Finney, Preface, *Systematic Theology*, quoted in Pratney, pp. 117-118.
[101] C.G. Finney, *Autobiography of Charles Finney*, quoted in Pratney, p. 121.
[102] Pratney, p. 122.
[103] Webster to Thomas Dawes, December 20, 1808, *Letters of Noah Webster*, Harry R. Warfel editor, New York: Library Publishers, 1953, Warfel, pp. 312-313.
[104] Chauncey A. Goodrich, "Memoir of the Author," *An American Dictionary of the English Language* by Noah Webster, Philadelphia: J.B. Lippincott & Co., 1860, p. xxii.
[105] Ibid., pp. xv-xxii.
[106] This story and quotes are from Peter Harvey, *Reminiscences and Anecdotes of Daniel Webster*, Boston: Little, Brown, and Co., 1877, pp. 412-421.
[107] Ibid., p. 414.
[108] Ibid., p. 419.
[109] Ibid., pp. 420-421.
[110] Ibid., p. 421.
[111] The translation of these verses is a combination of the KJV and NASV.

Our Mission

Transforming Culture for Christ: Training Leaders, Discipling Nations. The Providence Foundation is a Christian educational organization whose mission is to train and network leaders to transform their culture for Christ and to teach all citizens how to disciple nations. Since our inception in 1983, we have been work-ing to fulfill Christ's commission to "make disciples of all nations." Such nations will have transformed people and transformed institutions — family, church, and state.

Website: **providencefoundation.com**
Phone: 434-978-4535
Email: info@providencefoundation.com
Mailing Address:
Providence Foundation
P.O. Box 6759
Charlottesville, VA 22906